thank you for reading...

MISTAKES
IN THE
BACKGROUND

Most of my life has been building up to the day when somebody would take me **seriously** enough to publish my writing.

Now that this has actually happened I'm obviously relieved but also anticipating the out come, worried, surprised but most of all the most excited I think I've ever been since... I thought I lost my i-pod and then I found it hidden in the Buckaroo box above my wardrobe— well—that's not strictly true—this is _far_ better than that, but that was a very good day.

My name is Laura Dockrill. I am a poet and illustrator from South London and this will be my first published piece of work. Thank you.

WHAT ON EARTH?

This book is dedicated to risktakers, those who follow their instincts (that's brave) and to anybody who has done what they were told they couldn't do. congratulations.

There was a point in her life when
She actually thought She liked

riding a

bicycle.

But then she got a rash, on
her earlobes mainly.

Be the other one.
The bigger one.
The bolder one. The braver one.
The one that calls back, that asks on dates, that makes the choice, that finishes the milk, that uses all the hot water up. that takes the blame, that rips the mates top or at least sweats really badly in it. Be the captain, cook your tea in the microwave - (I mean your dinner.) Do what ever you want - you can you know, you don't have to tell everyone that they are "looking well." Have the last chocolate - the one that everyone wanted. Even if it's strawberry or coffee... or liquer... or out of date. EAT IT. Do draw a moustache on your face for work - be the one that taps your pen at meetings. HURRY UP. Say sorry. Be the world changer, the closet arranger, the pisstaker, the start over, the fall-asleeper-on-the-tuber-to-last-stopper-and-not-get-offer. Refuse to fake tan, don't wear "BECKY'S GETTING MARRIED, LONDON CHICKS ON THE PISS UP 2008!" top. Just don't wear it. Why? Be the investigator. Pay the bill, accept the predictable, learn an instrument - even if it's just the recorder. Snore. Wear boxers, shower in cold water, change your mind, Don't dress up at the fancy dress party. Say "Shutup!" expect it back. Sugar sandwiches. Never say never. "yes your arse looks fucking HUGE!" "sorry about earlier - I was a bit brash." Don't save cash. Take your top off at the beach. Leave it on in the pubs. Have 3 courses and enjoy them. leave the restaurant. Say "love", Say "Hate". Don't say "RANDOM." Crunch ice. Own up to having nits. I had them when I was little. It was rubbish. But it breaks the ice when making new friends. Something to talk about isn't it?

Sweetly

In the deep stretches of the pond-life stroke, the blushes and blooms of pretty flowers spray against drainpipes, diggers, fish and dives

Hears you beating thumps in her sleep- the tennis- stuck the cd in the gap- trapped the door on repeat. Her feet- blue- as if stiff elasashic bands had stolen her blood and run away with it.

Everybody scratched and pecked and scribbled. Days at the one' o clock club- the space-hopper, the plastic peas, the doll with the loose eye.

Stages of this clap out chapters of her text, the dialogue, the direction of this film flickering in her head. Where it has started, where it will end.

Shapes in the pillow plumped, dips in the springs warmth in the wraps of cloth and imagining chewing china, the mis-place of bones, apples on ice-cream cones and hums on the tone of tuneful drowze and puffed eyes smeared with gel and jelly funk.

Couldn't tell you where she was this morning.

Had she even woken up?

Should she breathe in or breathe out—

Or simply just give up?

Safe. The time ticks for structure - of pockmark mates
and dates without flowers, maps and swords and deserted
ships.
Her lips. His eyes. The butterflies.
Speaking of lips, she spat out in words that cracked and ached her
lungs and answered back and drowned weeds that tumbled slack and went
right back to the hairs on her arms, the days inside, the bruises on
his knuckles.
And still - under the window sill - the heart always thuds.
Knocks the brickwork, drips again into the pond,
Judders of her unhappy life, pupils, dancing madly behind her eyelids -
She sees the sea, the sky, grass, fruit and wheelbarrows.
Then. Ten tender drops of light urge her to yawn, break open her
eyes and cracked lips, rip her hips from sheets and crumbs from
biscuits.
The swell of darkness frazzles to a smoky mist, the
sunshine pours in and gives her face a kiss - yet - still
in her mind - afraid to be alone or left behind - she
waits as the flashbacks buzz back
mind spins, tangled flipbook webs, shadows over and over inside
of her head.
Where there is no real monster under her bed.
Mouth is wide open, thanks to a friend.
When all she ever wanted was a boy, a girl and a cat called
Benjamin.

A TRAGIC TALE OF TWO SPOILT SISTERS

I could sit here and write it all out, the facial expressions, the fury, the anger and dispute but need I really say anymore? except... my sister STINKS!!

No and YES

were invited to dinner,
YES is quite large - No is a tad thinner
and here, over pie they argued the share-
(No liked the pastry and Yes preferred the Pear)
But Yes always won over fights such as this
For she could laugh and grunt and take the piss
But over the pulling and shaking of the dish
No could only say "No" and Yes could only say...

And so the host of the party, of all of his guests
saw a quite pointless argument and gave
the whole pie to Yes...

"is that better?" the host asked-
"NO" said No and "YES" said Yes.
"Well I'm terribly sorry, Yes give No the rest!"
Yes peered down at her plate...
there was none left.

Yes...

Specks

I never realised you were so brave, but when I did I told you all the time.

All 3 of us, used to sit all smudged up together, arms pressed so that a sticky slip ~~wove~~ attached us. 2 sisters. 1 brother.

I liked to laugh at your teeth, push your bruises in, lick the tops of your biscuits and gleefully watch you eat them (without realising.)

Once we put you on the coathanger, through your t-shirt and hung you up on the back of the door. 19 minutes you were up there. Broke a record. The wood snapped. You cried when you hit the floor. "You should have known better Laura-Lee."

You taught me the Gameboy, said I was "OK" for a beginner. In the past, aged 2½, you were excited by a rocking chair. Went backwards and forwards like a pendulum incased inside a grandfather clock. You fell too far back.

Smacked your head onto the kitchen floor, wailed like a violent siren to hospital where they stitched you like a butterfly. Afterwards, the carseats fabric all blood drenched and flakes in your wool-like hair.

I couldn't bear anything to happen again.

AND now so tall, you can spell the word "disintegrate" and know all the words to "Shaun of the dead" my speck your taste is impeccable. I am impressed.

"Why am I So Stubborn ??? "

She asked, ramming her fingers into the jar of silver skinned onions- all the glossed up and slippery, made her thumbs numb and vinegary-
a food that bit back... HARD.
"Perhaps" said her mother,
"you were once a pickled onion yourself-
forever avoiding to be jarred."

My pain au chocolat.
My friend.

With my sisters favourite food
I have indeed met my match.
Two dark black thick streams
running through tunnels -
collapsed.
So dense and direct. Perfect.
Your fragile shell gets me aswell,
incased, so papery as delicate as
the jacket on a ladybird.
As you lie as snug as a bug in
a rug, I can't wait to pick you
up, amongst your mates in the
wicker basket, in the supermarket-
I eat you going round aisles,
forget about everything I have to do
for a while,
and get awfully jealous of the
French.

Heaven knows

I married when I was young–it seemed obvious at the time - I needed the picture to fill the image of the frame I had in mind. I had considered dentistry but clearly a working life was not the path for me, you see... the difference between you and me is that you've got no kids and I've got three:

Tilly

Abacus

and

Geoffrey

and the days whistle by in my pre-cleaned home and I've got one of those "in-house filipinos" as I couldn't manage on my own, I've got to do things like get to the gym...

stay slim, let the cat out and let him back in again...

Come on then Tobias!

Meow

I've got to throw out my winter wear, get in some summer gear, get Geoffrey a new haircut as he's nearly in his first year. And that is a whole thing all together. That means, as a mum, I must be... **CooL**!

So I've got to really do my research. I've got
to really jazz-it-up. I've got to know who
breaks it down and who the fuck rocks it up.
Smiths was my best bet

"Okay kids in the car,
right from the start!
I am the firefighter-
the helpful firefighter
la la la la la la."

I was as anxious and as curious as a cat.
I went straight past gardening, health and
well being, past home and antiques- I didn't need
all that - and to the magazine section, and
there I stood. Bemused. Shell-shocked.
Some geeky little braceface peers over my
neck and says...

You alright there mate?

Mate? mate? I'm not your mate... I mean
Yeah sure man bruva, I really need
to get my filthy paws on like a New Musical
Expressed...

I could see he was impressed,
and reached for the magazine
(slightly to the left.)

It was right of course it was - the best thing
I had ever seen. This was going better than I
thought and it smelt like the spirit of Teens.
And then, back at my "yard" how i learnt and
discovered,
this dark tragic kingdom that soon uncovered -
and opened its arms out to me.
I was embracing Joe Strummer, Shane Mcgowan
and his grandson - Pete Doherty.

At the hairdressers we sat
down Geoffrey.
"Make him look like
Johnny!" i laughed.
"Johnny who? Travolta?" she quaffed.
"Oh you know Mr Borrell, Mr Golden
touch, Mr fall and woops I've stumbled -
Wahoho - Panic in America!"
She clearly didn't care so the conversation got
boring but we got his hair all knocked up and shaggy,
like a crack-headed punk it was dyed black and
scruffy and then i thought "Well, seeing as though i'm
here, i might as well get a bit of breaking up done myself..."

Siouxie and the banshees eat your heart
out. For I was "Summin' else!"
Straight after that did a bit'a shopping,
Online of course, got Geoffrey and I tickets
to see the Strokes at ULU, of course,
STANDING.
But no matter how I masked it, it made
no difference-
the gig was a deadline and things were
about to get vicious. Sid.
Picking up the kids was no longer a
chore - it was just a bloody good cat-
walk

Lightspeed champion

Oh hi Lisa D's MUM - fancy seeing
you here. Where you off to tonight?
Cos' I'm just about to go
watch the killers - I'm such a
victim. Sick. Did you watch
Skins last night? it was so
"obvs" about chris and
Jal. Sale on at HMV, gotta get your arse down there
biatch. Heard the new kooks album, its kook-ing up a
storm. I'll send it over to you via Mp2. Got a myspace?
I have, add me-you'll be punished if you don't - just
type in WWW. MySpace. com/the cool mom - mom as in
American.

PEACE UK
NUME

And now I've sold my Filipino, I've sacked my cleaner,
We just have the house a whole lot more laid back
and touch more greener

Work doesn't really get
done whilst I'm spitting
in the mic,

TRY TO MAKE ME GO TO WAITROSE I said NO NO No!!

Pick up my telecaster and jam it out at night.
Express myself a bit, dust just sort of sits about the
house -
because I'm messing with i-tunes, watching Mighty
Boosh and drawing pictures on my shoes - and my
old friends don't believe me! They think it's
just a phase - so I <u>made</u> them believe me
with this Venus Razor Blade
and I was never one for self
harm but I was so passionate
about this I engraved "4 REAL"
on my arm.
Life was dull,
So bleak and
unhappy - I
Went to American
Apparel and did a bit of
retail therapy...

HEAVEN KNOWS I'M MISERABLE NOW...

4 REAL

PEGGY WHO?

I couldn't wait to get home and see Geoffrey.
Maybe we could write a song - put it on our
blog - maybe we could beatbox to the cat,
whistle the Ramones to the dog

But my whole entire house
was quiet,
   and on the kitchen table
was a note that said:

MUM, YOU'RE A TRY HARD
IT'S DRIVEN US MAD
I CAN'T TAKE YOUR BULLSHIT ANYMORE
WE'VE GONE TO LIVE WITH DAD.

GEOFFREY
(Tilly & Abacus)

Why its so good to hang out with Aladdin.

When in Paperchase, the bar, the cinema
I'd like him to steal me a microwave,
a jam jar, a wind-up car.
Point out the bits i'd like the most
then get involved in something else,
then up the sleeve, in the pocket
its like a disease- you want it-
hes got it
Such fast hands,
Slippery like butter
no need to matter an utter as it always

Comes home to mumma

Wrapped up in shiny paper
and then it belongs to me .

These are my bollocks and this is my stool, I'm taking it. Night.

Tambourine:

She grew up in one of those places where the lift stank
of piss-ing down with rain outside she watched her old
man ruin the face of the next door neighbour. A bust
lip and a smashed nose and left his ear hanging often
she would wonder why she was born into this world-
where her mother cooked a roast dinner from a
packet and nobody in her family even liked music

ally she was incredible, she had ears like a hound
her brain was like a satellite or a dictionary for
sound. She could recognise voices on the telephone and
eventually learnt visitors door knocks and could tell
by the bite of the crunch in the apple if it was Granny
Smith, pink lady or cox.
She knew the TAP
                                TAP TAP
of the PITTER, PATTER, POP
of her auntie's 8-year-old blue flip-flops and simply
said without a sound in her head "Think you need some new
shoes." She could tell by breath when it was close to death,
so she kindly informed her grandfather, she said "I think
it's best if you have a long rest because your life is
nearly... Over- but most of all - in addition- to scrapes of
toast, brushes in paint or the sound of popping bubble wrap-
was not the strum OF THE GUITAR, the bling of the harp...

but the percussion in her lap.
She loved the

TAM TAM TAM
of the tambourine   and   the

BANG BANG BANG
of the drum. If a song had no
TAM of the rine or **BANG** of the drum then
it simply was not a song.
She loved the tam, tam, tam of the rine
it was the tam, tam, tam of the rine,
and put together with bells and skin it
became her favourite thing.

Wax stain

She is making her mind up, making decisions,
wearing not a ~~stitch~~ stitch of knicker,
with her untouched cigarette that lonely whispers smoke,
in the ashtray - taking up space.
She is thinking about who reads the traintimes at the
trainstation - who does the voice belong to?
She is thinking about her left over left flip flop that she
left behind at the festival, the loser on X-factor,
the one that everybody said would make it,
the one that even did an interview - it was a fix.
Without an umbrella (it got snapped up in the weather and
was furiously shoved into the neighbours hedge...) she
looks forward to the evening -
Show off to her date that she can use chopsticks and
dagger him whilst he helplessly searches for a waiter to
bring a fork or spoon.
She recently finished a spontaneous knitted teacosy for
no particular reason - for no particular person.
She hadn't even a teapot.

A BABY RABBIT.

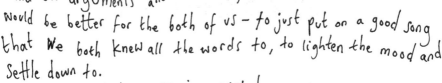

In this scientific world of us
and our arguments and noise and fuss
Would be better for the both of us — to just put on a good song
that we both knew all the words to, to lighten the mood and
settle down to.
WITH YOU it's always scoring altitude
and full of grit and attitude, and an avalanche falls down on you
like the crumble crunch of the Centre core breaking more and
more all around you.
With me it's always trying to be an easy breeze, acting like I was
thirty-three "TALK ABOUT THIS LATER CAN WE?"
And then I'm all hot bunned and cross
and shut-up tight like a jack-in-a-box
and lose my patience and lose my voice — and search for a
satisfying way to destroy-
Crush cups, crack chocolate phoneboxes, throw jars of Ragu in the
Supermarket — "I'm gonna buy it! I'm gonna buy it!"
Then when I waited to sift through the shit bits of it, beat off
like bats my bad thoughts that in my own made me want to do
away with this — be the revolutionist, push the pen back till it
S-N-A-P-S and quit. That's not it. Not with us-never it.
What a strong new backbone I have aquired-
my old one can move to Spain and retire
The way with you comes with arguments and jokes
but above it all strength, ourselves and hope.

dear miss winter,

when you first got your job at
the post office,
i was posting a letter to my sister
at college,
our eyes met over   liquorice and
newspaper,
and i watched your name on your
shirt, miss winter.

i remember wishing we had left
the shop together, wrapped up in
a parcel with letters of silly
bills and thank you notes of

please come again soon and no
i most certainly wont.
and us, like a small boat afloat
could drift away. and think about
making a home one day.
but obviously,

we did not.

from then on i just kept on
thinking about how much i loved
writing and that stamps really
were an excellent invention.
so i would come int to post in
hope of gaining your affection,

browisng over the fishermans

weekly or commenting that the
floor boards were SQUEAKY

and you, so fresh and pretty,

would sit and giggle quietly,

thinking that you were invisible
for all to see,
even though you were a lighthouse
to me.

its funny that they say patience is
a VIRTUE
as too many times this has
failed to be true,
but its my birthday next week and
i will be seventy two.

miss winter, you see, i have been
waiting for you since i was
seventeen,
am i too late for you-...

26th june 2007
dear incredible rolf harris,
i woke up this morning feeling awfully embarressed,
this is my 26th letter and you still have not responded,
its not my fault you are so great that my thoughts have been
bombarded by your indescribable ways
your connection with music,
 i have your signature on my wall so i never, ever lose it
ill never forget your didgeridoo
 im learning it still and have scraped a grade 2
 im gonna double up my lessons so i can be just like you
 i was in a band, so i can understand, how difficult it is to be

a struggling musician', hard to get your word out on the street
when nobody will listen
i play the keyboard, im grade 6
mum calls me stevie wonder, its a bit embarrising

i love playing the keyboard, i love stevie wonder too,

but i love you more

stevies shit compared to you

  youve made me vegetarian after your animal shows
  its actually rather easy but a bit awkward at home
  mum wont cook anything without rubbing a bit of meat around it
  i said mum, i dont eat that, im veggie like rolf
she said stop being so bloody difficult and do as you are told
 i adore your artwork
ive won some pieces at some auctions
ive got a big book at home, some of my own imitations of your
  excellent work
 i sometimes draw my friends, sometimes we all dress up and i
 play you for pretend
i wish i was you
i can dance you know
i could be everything about you
except for the beard because ,well obviously im a woman and that

would just be weird
saying that i have seen them in fancy dress shops
theres one on my highstreet, i pop in quite a lot

but i digress
its not about jokes, if it was a beard i was after
id like other blokes, but they arent all round artists .
and like i said ive captured all my friends as cartoons,
as caricatures
they all say yeah his are good but they arent as good as yours
oh and lookie here

im not the only one to notice youre so great
youve got a personal call to paint a royal portrait
and there you are

as quick as jack sticks to show off your art

up to bloody buckingham to paint the ageing tart

26 times rolf ive written to you

youve had your chance but now it has fled

it seems you think i were better off dead

you still wont paint me after all the things ive said-

ill tie myself kangaroo down sport instead.

I basically just think I should be the next Wonder Woman because I do more wondering about stuff than anyone I know. So it would work etc.

MAZes.

Utterly subliminal like the best bits of a black and white
film -
the mistakes in the background that not everyone has found -
You are -
treehouses and stuck in mud,
house of fun, steptoe and son, spaghetti
train journeys with a friend,
2cvs, Mercedes Benz - milkshakes and runaways to
Peru, Airwaves, Softmint, juicyfruit -
    The best ever cartoon...
Sunrays, breakaways, playdays, computer games, Bustamove,
Party tunes, Petit Filous and Timbuktu - Make believe and
fancy dress, hideaway den, a crows nest, tea in bed,
My favourite song on the radio - the volume, the fast
forward, the time to go -
Punk music, R'n'B and electro,
Pop, rock and roll, 2 step and disco - let's go -
to museums and waterparks
have a picnic in the park - in the dark,
play Connect 4 on Tower Bridge or just walk through
Mazes... or have you seen Labyrinth?
David Bowie - oh my gosh - he is sick yes?

Grapes from the fridge and Mini-eggs,
3D glasses and Right Said Fred,
French films, Red wine or Stars in your eyes -
What would you sing?
What would you sing?
Rap, maps of the world, hot sand, our land - before time -
that bit when the mummy long-neck dies -
i cried.
Popcorn - Salty or sweet?
Mix in Maltesers as a treat.
Four poster bed, you are a Mansion, a Houseboat, a Cave,
a Waterfall, you are glitter, a looking glass, a Know-it-all.
Popping bubble wrap, rearranging shelves and finding sea
shells, old park bench and jellied eels,
~~xxxxxxxxxxxxx~~ you have made up your mind there is no
going back.
You are soft seats, late night tv -
walks on cliffs and trampoline
drunkness and fruit and good smelling shampoo
Pomegranate seeds and crap tattoos
a team, strong tea, i'm proud of us
to see is like the relief of seeing the nightbus
Flowers that last much longer than you expected and
the pillow day so you don't ever have to go to work again!

The English language - I would say you're a good read,
Your mother's cooking, planting seeds
Hammocks, snow, thunder, hail,
Beetle juice, Thundercats, christmas, ale,
The Beatles, scooters, colouring in and Spring,
Hours, birthdays, dates and pads that cover the shin
when your rollerblading.
Acrobatics, dramactics, food fights, my bed side light
Oh my God you make me laugh -
My warm bath with plenty of bubbles that crackle like
rice krispies
SNAP!!
ice cream, on the roller coaster
picking the cheese off the inside of the toaster
coca cola with a marshmallow floater
dance for me - tap, anything, ballet -
float away like drunk from champagne -
then drink to piss the night away -
then sleep in hands the whole next day
Sunshine in may. Come to stay

ONE.
TWO.
THREE.
FOUR.
Happy DAYS.
You are the reason that I am weak.
Why I can't speak.
Now I sound like a fucking freak, I'm not, it's just that—
for the mind—you happen to be an absolute treat.

Pale.
So white as snow white as light as milk or
wedding silk so white you see...
the boys could see through her skin and through her coat
as white as white could ever be.
She finds scuttling through aisles, and her shoes slide
about on the tiles, the pharmacy can only assist her
to decide which version of commercial she should buy -
the only one she was recommended is
the only one she cannot find...
TANNING. It takes time.
Ointment, pigment, press, mousse and
crumble, as if a pie, a dessert, a once
unheard mumble votes for her to choose the
spray. She checks her head and remembers
the advert from the other day and thinks
"Who the hell am i to judge if it
makes me as brown as fudge - I'll
take it and I'll pay for it, thank-you
very much..."
Hometime is bolognese from the microwave,
Hollyoaks a chat with a mate, and then
it's upstairs for music a shower and to
fade a new shade...

The oozing from the tube as she
watches the cream,
   trapped fake glow inside L'oreal have
created their own sun beams,
and then standing naked, rubbing in,
smoothes it, spreads it on her odd pale
skin,
smears it on her legs and lines, arrows,
angles, rubs and changes-
isn't quite sure to include or ignore
her "whatdoyoucallit" places- still-
   all the while its brown smears marmite
like paste on her fingers, thighs,
wrists and ankles-
never knew until- she saw that this
was more than she could handle.
LOVE it never came easily.
She wanted to be handled desperately
but lies now like all the other wotsits
at the bottom of the packet-
nothing tanned about it-
        just an orange whatdoyoucallit.

The counter cools my arms and makes me think of home.
And the pinging ponging backwardsing
and forwardsing
of everyday ins and everyday outings.
You are nowhere to be seen on tv screens.
On radio pluggings or my window shuttings.
You ~~think~~ are not being read to me in bed. My book is so dull.

My book is so dull.
I couldn't give a...
surroundings
Its not even not being in your
I am just taken out of my surroundings and you're not
there.
And no matter how much sun-cream I use
no matter the brand, the advantages or the factor on the front
I smell you on my clothes
and I want to come home.

Manipulation

My good feet, my
My bad feet, my good
feet could kill me, they
Me, try to slip, trip up
Knee to the step to the
to the knee, you've got
boney, moany walk too slowly feet
always carefully, over any road that
by magically, tip-toed especially
I've got rough skin in places I never
toes-so knotted and twisted ...
Cock and my feet stop and I wait..
CHIROPODISTS emergency and who
these feet off of me? I've found
different shapes and sizes, from
Crisis! Minus the comfort-everyone
foot. Well no 'NAH DARLIN'' you have no under
Made is huge enough to fit a fruit underneath
hill or Haywards Heath. fitting into pretty
butters sisters! I've got corns, ingrowth bulks and
Pincers, my choppers, my dancers my heel-toe

# of my Sole

ad feet, my good feet,

feet, my bad feet, my own

cock up my hips and bruise

make a show of me...and its...

step

inturned, upturned, flat, crap and back-burned,

. . . .

I thought I was walking properly, treading

ever crossed me and now suddenly, as if

: they have let me down in front of me.

knew existed, I've got tough skin on my

and my knees lock and my heels

patiently. I am a patient at a

the fuck do I pay to see to get

my flippers cramped into shoes of

vintage to Reeboks, flip-flops to clogs to absolute

assumes to live its alright to have a pain in your

study its the only pair you have got. The shape I've

ontop you could picnic it, or frisbee it like on primrose

size 3s - Hold on tight - its a squeeze - I'm like Cinderellas

blisters - I've mistreated my steppers, my hoppers, my pokers

prancers and have no-one to blame but me.

Heart Poem

My heart.
    My heart. is perfect and in tact.
It is just that bit magnificent and, that is my fact.
It is the same shape as a fist, and the same
size as a fist.
    as a fist
    as a fist.

And I gather how it feels and argue with it, get
pissed off with it and enchanted by it, it beats
fast when I'm angry, faster when I'm panicing and
uncontrollably when I like what i see.
    And on the left hand side of my heart, my heart
my tickedy-boom-heart is always pumping, pumping,
pumping. Through tubes- somebody named them
arteries- the blood here is always shiny new, brand new-
John Lewis bedsheets new - the Vampires and Mosquitos
like it the best, they use it in lasagne, drapped over
baked potatoes or just an accompaniment to bread.
Now i can see us before me, and then this ribcage around
me, fluttering like a bird you see, inside a cage inside of me.
    MY HEART PLAYS BEATS FOR YOU.

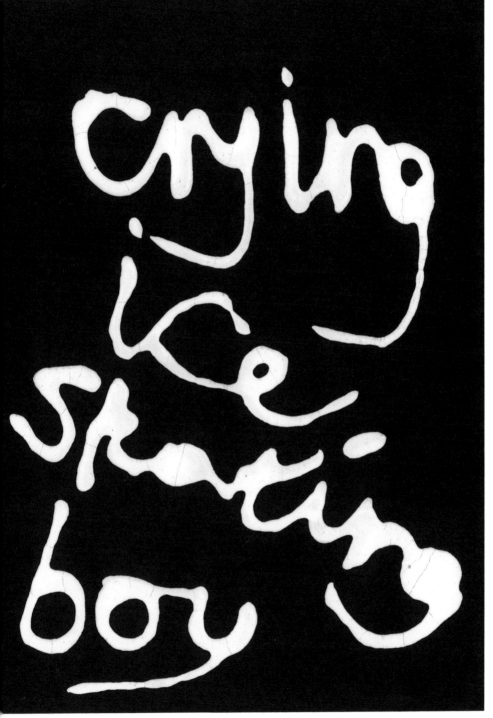

To understand the gravity of this heartbreaking tale, you must learn that little Horace came from a long line of fabulous, superb, championship figure skaters.

His grandparents, Marion and Samuel, were the world champions and the only couple to steal their title was none other than their very own daughter Florence and her husband Ned. Keeping the title in their name was obviously of great importance and so when Florence dropped onto her knees during a regular Sunday rehearsal (on the ice) - it was crystal clear that she and Ned were to be expecting the pitter patter of tiny skates.

The news made the papers - everybody could not wait to set their eyes on this new child prodigy. Once the sex was revealed, auditions were well on the way to find a suitable couple to create a pretty partner for Florence and Ned's son.

On the 6th of October out he popped - all screwed up like a spat out sweetie, clutched hands and heart beating so hard you could see it through his tiny chest.

His family cooed and gargled and saw the skating future in their arms as he was passed around his starry eyed family a cape of purple and gold was hung around his neck and little Horace was launched triumphantly into the air. Cameras snapped and fizzed all over him and the best skate boot maker was already scribbling designs down in the corner.

By four he was having regular rehearsals, missing days off nursery to spend time with Rebecca (his preferred partner) choreographing increasingly complex moves on the shiny dining room table.

By six he was taught at home by a lady with long teeth, who drew him pictures and smelt of coffee. In the evenings he would have to rehearse either alone or with Rebecca, going to auditions or attending events...

I'm making it sound like he was enjoying himself...

He wasn't. By nine years of age Horace hated nothing more than his ice skates. Second to that he hated the ridiculous dining room table in the ridiculous conservatory and last of all he hated absolutely everybody around him that made him do this absolute waste of absolutely all important time that was all his important time to absolutely waste if he so wished to do so. Horace liked to design. He liked shapes, lines and measurements and crunchy nut cornflakes and that was it.

Alone one evening, Horace had finished his evening rehearsals. His feet were sore and blistered and sat soothing themselves in a washing up bowl filled to the brim with salt and bubbles. He peered at the calender, only two months left until the

SKATES OF THE FUTURE

competition. He was dreading it. He was dreading it so much that he soon began to cry. He cried and he cried and he cried, fell asleep for a bit, and when he woke up he found himself in the middle of quite a surprisingly large puddle of tears.

His tenth birthday arrived. Horace was given the privilege to have no home schooling on this day, so he woke up at a drowsy 11.30, drenched from head to toe in what seemed to be water, he looked as though he had fallen into a swimming pool.

"What on earth has happened to you?" asked his pushy-nosed mother. "Have you wet yourself Horace?" asked his play-dough faced grandmother. Horace ignored them both and sloshed along to the fridge, his feet padding soggy trails along the kitchen tiles. This was the most Horace had ever cried (in one sitting at least). At the DINNER table that very evening his family expressed their excitement for the competition, debating the agility and style of the competitors and giving tips to Horace. Then, his father brought out from underneath the table a large square box. Then - for a second. For one tiny second Horace was curious. What on earth was it? It couldn't be something to do with design could it? He had skates, he had costumes - what if they actually thought about what he would like this year? HORACE pulled the box near to him and peered about the table. Everybody watched him, their eyes peeled back like soft-boiled eggs. He tore through the Galloned patterned paper.

SOLID GOLD SHEER
AVALANCHE 3
BLADE

And THERE they were. Like two unwanted bits of bad news. The ice skates. His mother dabbed a hankie around her eyes. "ENOUGH!" shouted Horace. "This has gone too far. I've had enough and I'm not doing it!"
"Oh yes you are you cheeky little sod, you haven't even thanked us for your skates!" His father warned.
"Because i don't want them! I hate them. I hate skating and I hate all of you for making me do it!"

The family gasped back in their chairs.

"Why you ungrateful, awful child, you've made your mother cry. Now get to your bedroom and don't come back until you have something nice to say."

Obviously Horace had nothing nice to say. So he stayed in his room for the whole evening, crying in his bedroom, he cried so much that his tears leaked down by the side of the radiator, through the floorboards and dripped through the ceiling, his grandmother put a pail down to collect them `THEM`.

He didn't stop there either. Horace successfully cried through the rest of the next two weeks building up to the competition, devastated that he had to go through with it and that his ignorant family couldn't see how unreasonable they were being. But the unhappier Horace became, the more forceful his family were. "You will stop crying and you will win this competition and be the blades of the future, if you embarrass us little boy... I'll make your life misery." his mother snarled.

Competition day came faster than microwave chips; Rebecca was at his house by 6.30 having her hair and make-up done by a lady from up the road (she had six dogs.) Horace refused breakfast. His grandmother pushed him into his Lycra costume, it was purple with gold vines creeping up the sides, and his cape went on to match.

"Do be the best today won't you son? Do it for the family." His grandmother whispered.

As soon as the pair stepped onto the ice the audience clapped frantically. Everybody recognised Horace from the papers but Horace could only sob into his cape. Rebecca shook his wrist "Stop it!" she hissed. But he just couldn't. He cried and cried, the auditorium dancing his wails around the ears of the crowd. Louder and louder. Rebecca threw her hairpiece out and stormed out of the rink. Disappointed, embarrassed and tired Horace just cried harder, so hard a voice went out on the speakers advising Horace to remove himself from the ice. But he was frozen.

It wasn't long before his tears began to soften the stubborn surface, warming it and moving it about before the hard icy disc snapped into several moving plates and Horace continued to sob. The sounds of the ice shards snapping was overwhelming, like elastic cracking back onto a sore thumb, clawing its way apart almost as though it were indulging in a well-earned stretch. Eventually the plate beneath Horace's feet shattered into tiny pieces and Horace fell into the freezing water, ice eating at his nerves. The audience, dumbstruck, sat and watched the poor ice-skating boy give himself up to the water.

His family, angry and exposed stood up. Tears streaming down their hard faces. That evening Rebecca was offered by her parents to give up skating in which she accepted gleefully and took up the guitar instead. Now older she works as a vet in Canada but did take the time to write a small note to Horace's family —

You can take an
Horace to ice.
But you can't make
him skate.
You handed him his
FUTURE on a platter.
But you broke his
Only plate.

THE SADDEST DAY IN
THE WHOLE ENTIRE
WORLD:

actually...
please turn over...

THE SADDEST DAY IN THE WHOLE ENTIRE WORLD IN REAL LIFE:

POPPYCOCK. This Life.

Like a massive seaside has s-t-r-e-t-c-h-e-d me
out and I can some TIMES , almost think that I might, just,
almost, maybe, quite, sort of, if I really strain, kind of if I look
like that, see the end. I can be the truck driver, the deep-sea
diver, the homocider, the life-saver, the man that sprinkles the cheese
dust on to the quavers, I'll be the greasy haired one that licks
the lids, eats the bigmac, the milkshake, nuggets on the side. I
want to shake like a snake on the dancefloor till I'm 94 - never be
underestimated. I can see colours, feel textures, understand the nectar
of this life. And it's POPPYCOCK! My washing machine eats socks,
my lightbulbs get eaten up by my dog, in the dark soul of the night it's
always four o'clock. The bus. The driver. The book. The shoe ontop of
the bus stop. The drain. The well. The wishing well. Now rich enough
to fulfill his wish and get that holiday to Brazil with a stop
over in Madrid. This nose-popping, hopping to hip, double bluffing,
windy breeze, teeth chattering, ever-evolving spinning
surface of POP and it's cocking. . . .
you idiot. i need a wee.

Refulgent

Insomnio: The area is that of a no-go, a conversation no no.

Finding it hard to sleep at night without a spout of light he flutters through the thoughts he thought he knew and leaks through panic sheets

And shadows stick to his skin like cobwebs and then gather around and drag him in - and he regrets the late night cheese again.

As he reaches the doors of the pool, he is soaked right through but the doors to the pool are shut.

Confused, he raps at the doors some more and fumbles with the lock.

He's the kind of man that isn't very kind, he likes the news a lot. He hates seeing people spill drinks down their chins, he likes to rub in shampoo, push his hair into a shark fin. He has 16 pairs of the exact same sock, he tries not to blink-a-lot.

2PM - the doors eventually split. Like the mouth of a beautiful lady inviting him in. The workers recognise him.

Inside. His cubicle offers him little service, advice or support. He showers cold. His feet are the shade of sick and cardboard. And still he would never get to sleep. No matter how many passing sheep or prints of feet he's prepared to see his imagination won't let him be.

As his ears drill underwater with his skill that some would describe as talented.

And the thoughts he thought he knew grew so tall they managed to stand up by themselves with no help at all... got so huge it was as if he had planted his own rainbows and forgot to notice all the ~~different~~ shades on the search for the pot of gold at the end.

Whilst swimming he hums the tunes his mother used to.

That make him think of warm afternoons.

Pimms, card games and garlic mushrooms

and 4 window dip, where there is that one called 'flavour pink'.

By 2.26 ...

He is dashing the racks, touching the sides with his big toe and then darting back,
of splash and the flecks speckled in his eyelash globs of water gob and no eye dust. No sleep.
And he is conscious of the ~~the~~ lanes, the time it takes,
and wish it were like a lullaby to lull him away or
make him a deadweight and sink like a big brick
bottom of the tiles— A seabed.
His alignment, vetebra, by vetebra, the drowsy ladder he climbs as though
he was stepping on the face of time, his bicep, the base of the back
and the spine.
Jumping Jacks, MISS MUFFETS cows, moons and spoons, walkers, ladybirds
and Poffins still swam in the way of his sky and _shill_ never would let him
sleep.
His bedside lamp has got cramp in all sides of the stand and insomniacs hands
bit the paper, the nails, the pillows the finger.
A swimmer. Not a sleeper.
And the Lanes. Repeat. Repeat. Re-peat. Almost sweetly sung the chime
that should be that of heavy breath and snore. Sublime—
The ins and outs of what rest is about — yet he cannot rest anymore.
_So_ in the lashing of wrave, in search for a place
he attempts to snooze in the depth,
Where the pressure is low, on the up-turned vertigo.
He would never again see another light breath.

You and Me and everyone else

I've bitten all my nails off again
it serves me right.
   I can't pick pennys off of tables, file
my nails or help to fish out splinters -
but in the winter I can wear gloves and never
get the wool caught.
   You love my fingers, my knuckles, my palms
my elbows, my knee-caps, my shoulders and my arms.
You haul me up-keep me calm
   like all-bran mixed in with lucky charms.
   Sweet. Keeping everything moving.
Now I'm getting like that jealous girl in school,
that leaves her bag and jumper on the seat on
the coach on the way to the swimming pool. I have
just got to sit next to you.
   Ring you on a tuesday "what you wearing this
wednesday?" Swap laces, swap shoes, swap socks,
you get pizza, I'll get pasta. Swap.
   Drink from the same cup.
I want to go to your house, borrow your pyjamas-

Smell like you.

Get all curled up and awkward,
around that radiator - do my spine in.
Wake up too early, whilst you have a lie in.
"Can I use your toothbrush?"
Drink from your tap, let you make me laugh and then
flop into your lap.

Eye up your mantlepiece and cut up cheese for you
into small squares and cook tea in the microwave
and make a mess and misbehave and never go away even
when we're making the other one a bit

Claustrophobic

I just wish that I could make us microscopic and
trap us in a snowglobe and set up home - without a way
out or even a housephone... let's stay in and eat this
out of date toblerone.

I want to use your mascara, pray we both get
an eye infection and sleep in your little room all day -
and eat meat and paint our faces.

I want us to be the spare set of cutlery -
two small teaspoons that everyone forgot about.
Sneak away to the back of the drawer and get
found dusty. Out of use.

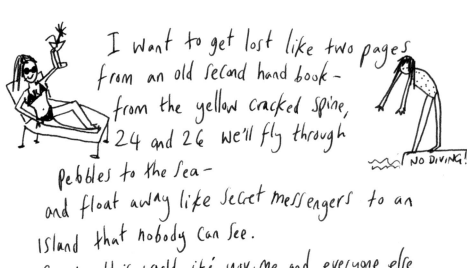

I want to get lost like two pages
from an old second hand book -
from the yellow cracked spine,
24 and 26 we'll fly through
pebbles to the sea -
and float away like secret messengers to an
island that nobody can see.
See in this world it's you, me and everyone else
it's disgustingly ugly - but it's the truth.
Our chess board, we are the pawns for only
eachother - you'll soon discover - I'd **lose** to
no one but you. My friend. My Queen.
    I adore
        you.

NO DIVING!!

smudge

My ~~Gran~~ Nanna doesn't like us coming round because we do so many naughty things,
We draw on the cabinets and hide her belongings and ~~[scribbled out]~~ go to the shops without telling her we're going. She purses her lips, puts her hands on her hips and says:

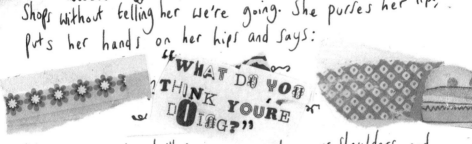

"WHAT DO YOU THINK YOU'RE DOING?"

But we know the drill by now and shrug our shoulders and get on with being annoying. She thinks we make such a "terrible riot", so much so, she follows us round with a dust pan and brush and a J-cloth.

Her house, so immaculate and so is her stuff... and that is what really irritates us. But one day-one of the ladies from the church made such a delicious cake, and our nanna ate it all and got chocolate all around her face- My brother laughed, my sister smirked- and I forgot to tell her...(by mistake)

Confess to me and say to me that you are not a leanover.
That in the mornings when the alarm clock gargles, knocker hits the bell and your strong
arm, all tense and definite leans over and gives me a kiss of chalky fuzz - you are
leaning over - are you not? Me underneath like a new monkey - "Ouch! you're on
my bloody hair again love!" Stay up late watching you, haunting the windows like
Bruce willis, marking the furniture, the street, the next seat on the train, in good
shoes, a paper under your arm, in a vest. I see you pick out tomatoes for me out
of packaged sandwiches and leave the teabag in for the right amount of time -
or lifting the bag off my chest to "give the boobs a rest."
Forbidding me, always, to do things - bite my nails, pick off the ringpull -
take no excuses, I'm always in trouble -
you think you are not the leanover, that leans over me like a big oak tree over
a small flower, I'm like the child in the cot, you like an onlooking proud
father -
        but as I get older - I will one day leanover you.

In a nut shell.

My love for peanuts
has rather, developed, you might say.
I was diagnosed with the allergy
when I was in nursery - I
unfolded the clingfilm in the book corner and found
peanut butter had clung to my cheeks in hives
on hotspots and gory nettlerash.
I had dare not go near them for years.
But since breaking up with my wife
and her moving in with the hunk monkey nut
from no.23,
a flight to New Zealand, left me
really wanting to live life on the edge.
So I occasionally indulge in a bag of KP
and fall unconscious onto the settee
Or sip any drink from any factory
that the ingredients might be quite near to or to go as
far to say that they may actually (woops I wasn't wearing my
glasses) contain some traces of nut.
And I'm out, swimming in a dream of cashew and pecan
atishoo - it's dangerous - but it reminds me I have guts.

S Q U A R E

The office.
Used to be a rectangle but has now been converted to an oval.
"We found the shape made our work environment ~~better~~ a much more sociable, and vibrant enclosure."
with deep padded, five star base, high, executive chairs that elevate up and shift down - and also swivel... around.

REMEMBER
REMEMBER
THE 17TH OF
DECEMBER-
XMAS BASH
@ HAHA BAR-
C'MON DOWN-
WILL BE A LAUGH.
R.S.V.P
Christin

FIG.
Nº 27

Oh, I love the work christmas parties- it's so fun to slip out of the suit and into something tarty- I go as Santa's helper and we all get pissed- it really is a great excuse to get fucked off my tits!

next
3%
20°

most accounts?

hilton
+ gray hound 1.com
@g...

736
921

=

And that's when Nigel spoke from across the
Oval office - all heads spun round electric
like the broken fuse from a socket.

different lens from this one

mums jumper

I ♡ Deer

high trousers

↑ socks and sandals

Socked and sandaled up
and cancer research tie.
a different lens for
different eyes but we
all assumed that he was
blind - mummy's jumper on
and his trousers were too
high - would have given
him the time of day but
quite frankly we'd ,
bigger fish to fry.

A fan of
BRAIN ATTACK
the worst program
on tv -
his tongue seemed to know
e-v-e-r-y-t-h-i-n-g
about
a-n-y-t-h-i-ng

Hi buddy!

Which made his breath smell sickly- He was out
of
the
ordinary

DANDRUFFED and scruffy,
beaky little face and jaw like he was
chewing toffee

Work christmas party
you say- i might just
drop by- course I'll have to
check the agenda with
brain attack and all- see if
I'm available that night...

Oh this isn't really
a party- more a
gathering
of the kind...

We all looked at eachother
nervously... we had lied-
what we really meant to
say was...

but we're far too polite here and most of us are actually quite shy.

christian →

"LISTEN MATE, we love ya' here - we think ya' bloody great - we don't wanna embarrass you or make a fuss but you are an embarrassment and just not one of us - us here at the office are fresh, fit and sporty and at the party - we'll be getting... NAUGHTY!

You dress badly,
  You're chunky and balding -
    You're only twenty-six, but you look as
though you're forty,
it's not just that you're unattractive - you just
stand Out - we're like chocolate, champagne and
sushi and well - you're a brussell sprout - soz' pal -
don't be annoyed... maybe they'll be another
work party going on somewhere you can join?"

=== **LATER THAT NIGHT** ===

Nigel drew a plan of action in
biro on his leg,
cut down his portions of bacon
and doubled up in egg -
He went to TopMan was kitted
Out by a stylist - baker boy
hat, levi jeans and got his
hair **high**lighted, shaved
his chinny chin chin and rollerbladed to the
gym - within weeks he was systematic, hydromatic -
      grease lightning!!

A writer sealed an envelope, popped into Nigel's pigeon hole with a post-it note saying

HEY YO Nigé -
Free 2NITO
nite? XMAS
bash at HAHA

2 Miss it
would be a
crime - looking
Pretty cool
these days-

Nigel saw the
note- and the invite
to the "do"- pushed his
N-SYNC fringe to the side, as you do,
and went home running to get ready
for the night-
he was really cool these
days-he was really cool alright.

MWAH
MWAH!!!
Christina
xxx

Come the next evening he gets a
text from the blokes-
asking him to put some cash **in** for a
couple lines of coke and just as he was
leaving there was an advert on **TV.**

beep
beep

BRAIN ATTACK
TONIGHT-
the entire trilogy-

BRAIN
ATTACK

Ooh i could
just watch
5 mins and that
will be me-
then it will be
off to HAHA to get
loose at a partay!!

But the clock kept ticking and his lips were twitching as he beat every contestant ~~aww~~ on the show that evening.

Christian at the party-
heart beating -
there was to be no sign
of Nigel at all this evening.

You won!

Nigel put on his Jimmy jams, sat back to relax, and won £50 over the phone on Brain attack -
it just goes to show you can take the geek to Topman it doesn't mean he'll turn out to be an absolute tosser.

My name is Ron. As far as parties go I am invited to... err... none about... Although last week my luck turned around when my cousin (twice removed) had a party in town. 1.

*I got a suit from for the blind and was given £1.50 off because the old lady was kind. She also said I looked handsome in blue. She obviously didn't realise that I was used to being lied to. (I couldn't help thinking that perhaps she was blind too.) 2.

I gave my twice removed cousin a clock from my shelf – because I could not find anything else. She liked it. It made me hate her a bit. I had a glass of punch, it got me a bit drunk because I only had Haribo for lunch. 3.

I really should stop doing that so much.

AAAH

4.

and then left.

The hours went by, sat in the same spot, glugging brandy from a teapot (there were no glasses left for me). An old man came over and asked who I was, I said I was "wassit-faces cousin" and my mothers name was Ro?. 5

That I enjoyed photocopying my head and hated my job, and would rather be in KFC eating corn from a cob. He recognised mum's name and my family tree and held his hand out to me, laughed and shook his bald head 6

and said there was a rumour going around that I was dead. I called him a dickhead- 7

I was happy when I managed to find a Co-op, and browsed around for crisps and dip or anything salty to stick my paws into. Queue up with Coke and Pringles – I couldn't help wondering if the cashier was single. Her eyebrows were waxed like small tadpoles, and her knuckle had its own mole – then I noticed that I had one too...oh no – it was just a bit of melted Twirl.

Would you like to go on a date?

Fuck off.

NEXT PLEASE

And handed me a receipt, which was sweet. Some people just slam it on the counter don't they?

Maybe that means she likes me.

MONDAY 8 AM

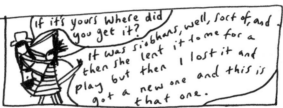

He's on a long ting son,
gotta go elsewhere if he wants some,
he can kiss me up but he won't get none –
this is when a girl gets called "No Fun".

Tonight is my bredwins' party,
I like his work mates 'cos they're bare arty
they care about more tings than just getting dirty
and they like me 'cos im well flirty...
              But whoo woops there he is –
              usher lookalike out on the
          piss –
    grinding up to some next mans
    missus should keep his hands to
himself i think –
Tasha, Shanika, Shanai and ~~mona~~ Mona,
think that the ~~the~~ breh's a begga
friend ~~loner~~ loner –
and bare dodgy 'cos he drinks Corona
but (I think i'll drink it too when
      I'm older – and more cultured
        'cos it's foreign... ain't it?)

Later as the party heats up
I'm sipping my rum from a paper cup
eyeing up the fly boys, dancing well rude
to some local boys garage tune.

Usher boy steps next to me—
whispers he wants to chat to me—see—
I was drunk and feeling silly—
everybody in the club getting tipsy.
He holds my hand well smoothly
and says he wants to move me
lists all the things he could do to me—
doggy style or me giving him a blow job
(and that was it really!)

"I like you, you know, I'll
take care of you girl,
take you on a magic
carpet
tripping round the world—
I love my ladies but you could
hold me down—come on cheeky
turn that frown upside down..."

I ain't got time for you boy 'Cos you chat out your arse why you always stepping next to me? You're too fass - can't you just leave it with things the Way they are? your face is always in my grill you need to fix up star.
I LOVE YOU GIRL!
NO YOU DON'T
I NEED YOU GIRL!!
SOON YOU WON'T
LOW ME GIRL- PLEASE I'M REAL- AIN'T A BREH ALLOWED TO EXPRESS THE WAY HE TRULY FEELS?
ABE
I love you

See this is when things get **Hard**, I need to tell you a story and it is **dark** - 'cos I had a pair of kickers that got jacked from my **yard** - some dog girl came over that I thought was my friend - she borrowed my crepes I never saw her again...

- liberties I know!!

3 years later and things are sick!
I'm living in Kennington and it's wicked!
Usher boys in jail for dealing (even though he don't
deal...)
but I've got a baby now— so at least I can
appeal ...

Next day in Brixton— in the hair shop—
I recognise some next girl I knew from Topshop—
She comes over to me, drags out my extensions
I thought she was on crack or craving attention—
but she blazes me boy— says I stole her man ...
Ushers her baby father and I was like

SLAM

I didn't believe her bullshit and I went to
Maccie D's —
and got a chocolate milkshake, and drank it on
my J's (Neekie)...
and then I realised it was probably true
Usher boy has got this reputation that I tried to
see through...

I finished my milkshake,
put my daughter in her buggy,
put a bit of milkshake onto her dummy—

Usher boy can stay in jail—
boy he's a loss—

but oh my days—
i got a promotion at
Argos!!

TEMPORARY
BUS STOP!

PLEASE BE AWARE THERE IS A PIGEON IN SCREEN NO 1

Found in the Streatham Odeon.

Ducks Day.

The duck is ill.
He is living in a box upstairs
filled with hay.

There has been talk
of duck for christmas,
I guess it isn't ducks day.

<u>And a bubblebath</u> ~~~~~~ <u>bottle in</u>
<u>the shape</u> of <u>Fireman Sam.</u>

Same eyes, a million eyes, a
million times
we've laughed over the same
stuck out bends in our lives
and our hair, in tangles, grew
from similar needles in heads
and the spots on our tongues
mirrored to the lines on our
fingers- touch the mark like
Doc leaves on nettle stings
and share the same bed,
Share the same breath-like
two small spiders sharing the
same web-and habits we have
and owned and lost and our
voices, the same - scare even me.
You're just me just smaller and
stranger and I'm just you just
bigger and WEIRDER and we're just
eachother just with lashes flapping
up and down in different scenes but
we're from the same set of
fruit and fell from the same barrell,
rolled down the hill and bruised
and worm trodden
and are still here,
and still have after all these years
the same eyes.

THE MAN WITH SUCH LONG ARMS...

by laura.

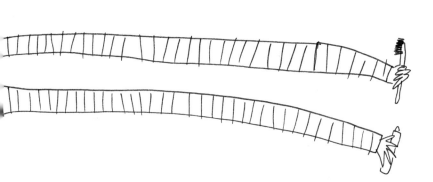

So brushing teeth
wasn't always
easy. The end.

You knew this boy from Primary School—
  he was always someone you really <u>felt</u> that you could
talk to—
  about filling up paper cups with ants and who could say the
alphabet and that...
  All the boys and girls would cuss and say you loved eachother
up but you'd just laugh and brush it off **and** get on with
picking your nose — or drawing pictures of your mum, or whatever
else you did in those days—
  You go to the same secondary school and things just are not
the same at all — everyone has to wear a schoolbag—
even a uniform.
He enjoyed himself though—he was 'popular' too...
in other words he went out with just about everyone except
for you, but its not as if you <u>asked</u> him—you just sort of
hung about—
Sipping a Sunny delight near where the rubbish was put out,
all the other girls wore bras and knew how to snigger,
you knew how to whistle and spit and stick up your middle finger,
Sometimes he'd ask you to wait, ~~and walk home~~
So the two of you could walk home together—
You'd be by the gate,
and he'd be off snogging some slut or whatever.
<u>SAD</u>. Seven years at school together and this is all you can
remember,
you blame him for your crap CV, its his fault you aren't that
                                                        clever—

What is he? An *artist* now? He goes to college and wears hats-
he has to have a portfolio to hoard all his crap,
he calls his tutor by her first name- fancy that-
Whilst he has the initials of an artist T.W.A.T,
he never calls you, he never texts you- he rarely comes over to your house,
mostly he just sits and smokes rollies in the park and "hangs out".
You'd like to "hang out"- you'd probably be pretty good at it- but he
never invites you- he couldn't give a shit.
In the daytime you take photos of passers by.
and make up stories about their lives
in the darkness of your bedroom- developing at night.
He has a girlfriend- or possibly three...
You don't mind at all though, you are through with jealousy.
At the bus stop, two years later, you wished you had a car,
You get a text, on a bright green screen- asking where you are.
Nervous, you get the 159 to the river where you get off and walk,
he buys you a burger at Waterloo, stabs you with a fork,
he cuddles you in chinatown, sings you a song,
you spill tea on his jeans in covent garden, list all the bits he got wrong,
You climb on his back at piccadilly- a short cut to leicester square
After pushing eachother into leaves and trees he says he wished he'd been
here- and then he holds your hand in Budgens (and that proves he
really cares.)
And now he leans into you, like the arc of an old tree,
over a house that's been there for **Life** and sits beautifully
in your hands he draws your future and the way that things will be.
It's not till years later, when you sit with furniture and kids
he pulls out twenty-eight paintings of you for each year and says-
            "I always gave a shit."

HARPER
An imprint of HarperCollins*Publishers*
77-85 Fulham Palace Road, Hammersmith, London W6 8JB

www.harpercollins.co.uk

This paperback edition 2008
1

ISBN-13: 978 0 00 730 0594

photographs for 'MAZES' by Joshua Osbourne
my photograph taken by Sonny Malhotra, make up by Jacqui Rathore

Printed and bound in Italy by L.E.G.O. SpA - Vicenza

Design by *'OMEDESIGN*

Mixed Sources
Product group from well-managed
forests and other controlled sources
www.fsc.org Cert no. SW-COC-1806
© 1996 Forest Stewardship Council

FSC

FSC is a non-profit international organisation established to promote the
responsible management of the world's forests. Products carrying the FSC
label are independently certified to assure consumers that they come
from forests that are managed to meet the social, economic and
ecological needs of present and future generations.

Find out more about HarperCollins and the environment at
www.harpercollins.co.uk/green

Alg. She is the
niece.

che
Uncle Joe f . .

THANK YOU...

To all of my family and friends
that have listened to me moan and
get stranger over the years, come to
my gigs, plays, parties, house for tea
and crackers - supported my ideas and
stood up for me, relied on me, trusted
in me and are still here today.
Thank you. These poems, pictures and
stories are for you.

love
Laura
xxxx

Fry the onion
the remaining
ld the tomato p.
to juice and
er for abo
and

15 thursday

拉
pull
拉
pull